HENRY PURCELL
THOMAS MORLEY
JAMES PAISIBLE
THOMAS TOLLETT

# Funeral Music For Queen Mary

(1695)

for SATB choir and organ, oboe band,
four slide trumpets, kettledrums and military drums

Edited and reconstructed by
Bruce Wood

Full Score/Vocal Score

NOV 072464

Novello

# CONTENTS

# INSTRUMENTATION

2 oboes
tenor oboe (or cor anglais)
bassoon
4 slide trumpets (or two trumpets [C or B flat] and 2 tenor trombones)
military drums
kettledrums
organ

*Duration: c.20 minutes*

Instrumental parts for the Marches and the Canzona are available on hire or for sale to special order from the publishers.

*The Funeral Music For Queen Mary (in Bruce Wood's edition) is recorded on Collins Classics 14252, performed by The Sixteen and the Orchestra of The Sixteen, conducted by Harry Christophers. It is also recorded on Sony Classical Arc of Light SK66243, performed in Westminster Abbey by the Abbey Choir with the New London Consort, conducted by Martin Neary.*

# HISTORY AND BACKGROUND

A fully documented account of the research which resulted in this publication is given in my article "The first performance of Purcell's Funeral Music", in *Performing the Music of Henry Purcell*, edited by Michael Burden (Oxford University Press, 1996). A digest of its main points is given here.

Purcell's celebrated anthem "Thou knowest, Lord, the secrets of our hearts", composed expressly for the funeral of Queen Mary in Westminster Abbey on 5 March 1695, cannot have been sung alone on that occasion, for its text is not an autonomous portion of the Anglican funeral liturgy, but merely the concluding section of what in his day was termed the "second dirge anthem" - the group of funeral sentences specified by the rubric in the Prayer Book "to be sung at the grave".

There is clear documentary evidence that, at state funerals in Restoration England, Thomas Morley's setting of the Funeral Sentences was customarily sung - but sung incomplete, for his setting of the sentence "Thou knowest, Lord" had been lost earlier in the century. (It was not to return to circulation until the late eighteenth century, when it was published by Boyce, his source being a privately owned manuscript.) Purcell's "Thou knowest, Lord", long admired for the purity of its antique style, perfectly matches Morley's setting of the remaining Funeral Sentences in key, metre and texture, and in being notated with a minim rather than a crotchet pulse even though it is in common time - a combination almost unknown elsewhere in Purcell's music. Yet it is by no means pure pastiche: Purcell's harmonic language is more intense than that of a century earlier. Indeed, according to Thomas Tudway, the expressive eloquence of the piece drew tears from the entire congregation at the Queen's funeral.

The music for the procession in which the Queen's body was borne to Westminster Abbey has been assembled from various sources. The two oboe marches were published some months after the funeral, in an anthology of pieces aimed at the amateur market; it may well be that their note values were halved for this purpose, since they are half those of Purcell's March for slide trumpets, which remained unpublished. It is preserved - together with his Canzona, which was played during the Queen's interment - in a manuscript whose copyist helpfully indicated the exact function of both pieces: the March is headed "Sounded before her Chariot" (that is, the horse-drawn royal hearse), and the Canzona "As it was sounded in the Abby after the Anthem" (that is, after Purcell's "Thou knowest, Lord". The Canzona thus accompanied the elaborate ceremonial associated with the interment of the Queen's body, when officers of her household formally broke their white staves of office, and cast them into her tomb together with the keys and badges which were their other emblems).

The origins of the Old English March for military drums are shrouded in antiquity; it probably dates from the sixteenth century or even earlier. In 1632, lately revived, it was prescribed by Charles I as the only march to be used by the infantry. It is also the only march included in the manuscript notes for Randall Holme's *Academy of Armoury*, published (though without the projected chapter on drumming) in 1688 - a fact which points to its continued exclusive use in the Restoration period. It is, indeed, the sole English drum march to survive from the seventeenth century or earlier. Although no account of the Queen's funeral bothers to mention it specifically, it is highly likely that this march, distinguished by what Charles I's warrant describes as its "ancient gravitie and majestie", is what the 30 military drummers who took part in the procession would have played. That they *did* play, rather than carry their drums in silence, there is clear evidence; one eye-witness account of the procession graphically describes the sound not only of drums but also (corroborating the evidence contained in the manuscript of Purcell's March) of trumpets.

Documents relating to the funeral record the provision of two funerary covers for kettledrums. There is no evidence that these instruments were played in the procession, or even carried in silence, but an eye-witness account of the service in the Abbey describes hearing "the sound of a drum unbraced" - that is, one with its head slackened in the traditional funerary mannner - during the actual interment. (On other state occasions such as coronations, kettledrums played in the Abbey with the royal trumpets; military drums, however, remained either outside the Abbey or at Westminster Hall.) An editorial kettledrum part has accordingly been added to Purcell's Canzona.

# PERFORMANCE

## *The processional music*

The appropriate instrument for the Old English March is the military drum - not unlike a modern orchestral tenor drum; in the context of a funeral the snares would have been off and the head slackened somewhat. Contemporary standing orders stipulated that processional drumming be uninterrupted. At least two drummers were assigned to each company of infantry; each of them was permitted to rest occasionally, but the other was required to continue in the meantime. The Old English March should thus be repeated without a break while the oboe and trumpet marches are played. An appropriate tempo is around 54 to the minute (minims in the drum march and the Purcell March, crotchets in the oboe marches). This pulse corresponds not to a complete marching step but to the "half-step", in which the forward-moving foot momentarily pauses alongside the one on the ground: a traditional feature of the dead march.

English regimental oboe bands in the 1690s numbered twelve players: three each on first and second treble, tenor, and bassoon. Such numbers made it unnecessary for Paisible and Tollett to confine themselves to short phrases separated by rests, whereas Purcell, composing a trumpet march to be played one-to-a-part, was obliged to make careful provision for the players to breathe. In the march by Paisible the meaning of the tied pairs of minims is unclear; it may indicate a gentle re-articulation, without tongueing, of the second note in each pair. Soft articulation of repeated notes - a traditional feature of funerary wind music - may also be what is denoted by the marking "Tremulo" in the manuscript of Purcell's Canzona, though the exact position in which that word is written there - not above any of the staves, where a performance direction would normally be inserted, but in the left-hand margin adjacent to the second and third trumpet parts - leaves a suspicion that it may be nothing more than an amplified misreading of "Trum" (for "Trumpets") in the copyist's source.

## The choral music

The Anglican Service at the Burial of the Dead includes what are generally referred to nowadays as the seven Funeral Sentences. These are grouped into three portions of text, which in the seventeenth century were termed the three Dirge Anthems. The first anthem, consisting of the sentences beginning "I am the resurrection and the life", "We brought nothing into this world", and "In the midst of life", is directed in the Book of Common Prayer to be sung by "the Priest and Clerks meeting the corpse at the entrance of the Church-yard, and going before it, either into the Church, or towards the grave". After one or two psalms and a lesson there follows the second anthem, consisting of "Man that is born of a woman", "In the midst of life", and "Thou knowest, Lord"; this is directed to be sung "when they come to the grave, while the corpse is made ready to be laid in the earth". (At the Queen's funeral in 1695 it was after the singing of this anthem that Purcell's Canzona was played.) After a short prayer of committal there follows the final anthem, "I heard a voice from heaven".

It was customary in the Restoration period for Tudor and Jacobean music for full choir to be accompanied on the organ even if the vocal parts disclose a complete harmonic texture, and Morley's setting of the Funeral Sentences is no exception. Purcell clearly intended his setting of "Thou knowest, Lord" to be accompanied on the organ, since at one point (bars 130-131) the vocal bass line is independent of the continuo bass. In addition the piece was, as Thomas Tudway noted at the head of his transcription, "accompanied with flatt mournful trumpets" - the four slide trumpets doubling the voices; they probably did so not in order to add colour, but primarily to warm up discreetly before playing the difficult Canzona. They may have been obliged to re-tune after playing in the funeral procession: the pitch of regimental oboe bands in the 1690s is unknown, but that of the Abbey organ, rebuilt only a year or so previously, seems to have been about A = 453 - a quarter of a tone above modern pitch.

# THE ANGLICAN FUNERAL ORDER

¶ *The Priest and Clerks meeting the corpse ... and going before it into the Church ... shall say, or sing:*

I am the resurrection and the life ...
I know that my Redeemer liveth ...
We brought nothing into this world ...

[*Then follows Psalm 39 or Psalm 90, or both, and the Lesson (1 Corinthians 15, vv. 20-40)*]

¶ *When they come to the grave, while the corpse is made ready to be laid into the earth, the Priest shall say, or the Priest and Clerks shall sing:*

Man that is born of a woman ...
In the midst of life we are in death ...
Thou knowest, Lord, the secrets of our hearts ...

[At this point in the service Purcell's Canzona was played.]

¶ *Then, while the earth shall be cast upon the body ... the Priest shall say* [*the prayer of committal*].

¶ *Then shall be said or sung,*

I heard a voice from heaven ...

[*Responses, prayers, a collect and the Grace conclude the service.*]

[The order of service as given in the Book of Common Prayer makes no provision for a sermon, but at Queen Mary's funeral a sermon was preached by the Archbishop of Canterbury, Thomas Tenison, before the final responses and prayers.]

# LIST OF SOURCES

*The Old English March*

**TF¹** T[homas]. F[isher]., *Warlike Directions: or the Souldiers Practice* (London, 1634), pp. 5-6. The March is printed in a letter-based mnemonic notation, without specific indications of rhythm: | for a right-hand (strong) stroke, **I** for a left-hand (weak or anacrusial) stroke, **r** for a ruff (or roll), **2** for a half-ruff (or flam); the end of each phrase is marked by a full stop.

**TF²** Second edition of the above (London, 1643), pp. 5-6.

**RH** London, British Library, MS Harl. 2034, ff. 75-76: manuscript notes, in the handwriting of Randle Holme, for his *Academy of Armoury* (Chester, 1688). Holme gives the opening Voluntary in both mnemonic notation and staffless notes (crotchets, minims and semibreves), but the March in mnemonic notation only. His mnemonic is based on syllables, not letters: **pou** (right-hand stroke), **tou** (left-hand stroke), **pong** (stroke falling at the end of a line), **rou** (ruff); there is no indication of the half-ruff.

**HW** Horace Walpole, Earl of Orford, *Catalogue of Royal and Noble Authors* (London, 1759), 200-202. The Voluntary and March are printed in staff notation, in the same note-values as those given by Holme, and "underlaid" with very similar mnemonic syllables.

*Paisible and Tollett: Oboe Marches*

Published in *The Sprightly Companion* (London, 1695), unpaginated: items 18 (Paisible) 19 (Tollett). Both pieces are printed in parts, not score.

*Purcell: March and Canzona*

Oxford, Oriel College, MS UA 37, unfoliated, last item (unique source: score, c. 1700, in the handwriting of an unidentified copyist).

Purcell included a slightly different version of the March in his incidental music for Shadwell's play *The Libertine* - almost certainly for a revival during the remaining months of 1695, for the theatre version shows clear signs of being an adaptation of the funeral version and not vice versa. The theatre version is preserved in several sources, the earliest among them being Cambridge, Fitzwilliam Museum, Music MS 119, and London, British Library, Add. MSS 5333 and 31447.

*Morley and Purcell: Dirge Anthems*

Primary sources

**A**    Oxford, Bodleian Library, Tenbury MS 859, pp. 1-11 (score, c. 1730, in the hand of an unidentified copyist; complete; headed on cover *The Buriall Service / Dr Morley*; bars 110-135 have no separate attribution).

**B**    London, British Library, Harl. MS 7337, ff. 174v-177 (score, 1716, in the hand of Thomas Tudway; lacking bars 110-135).

**C**    London, British Library, Add. MS 5054, ff. 128-133v (score, c.1760, in the hand of Henry Needler; attributed to Morley and Purcell in table of contents (f.2), and to Purcell at bar 110 (f.132); lacking bars 136-156, for which Croft's setting of the final sentence is substituted, without attribution). Needler's source from bar 110 onwards appears to have been Croft's *Musica Sacra*; variant readings of **C** in bars 110-135 have accordingly not been listed in the Commentary.

**D**    London, British Library, MSS MadSoc A52-55 (set of part-books, c.1730, in the hand of an unidentified copyist: Treble, pp. 146-152; Countertenor, pp. 140-146; Tenor, pp. 135-153; Bass, pp. 124-130. Lacking bars 110-135, whose place is occupied by Morley's setting of the sixth sentence.)

**E**    Oxford, St John's College, MS 315, pp. 215-218 (organ-book, c.1665, in the hand of Edward Lowe; lacking bars 110-135).

**F**    London, British Library, Add. MS 31444, ff. 208-208v (score, c.1705, in the hand of an unidentified copyist; bars 110-135 only).

**G**    Oxford, Christ Church, MS 794, ff. 1-2 (score and separate organ part, c.1700, in the hand of an unidentified copyist; bars 110-135 only, headed on f.1 "Mr Hen: Purcell's Part of the Buriall Song").

**H**    London, British Library, Harl. MS 7340, ff. 264v-265 (score, 1717, in the hand of Thomas Tudway; bars 110-135 only).

Secondary sources

*Bars 1-109 and 136-156*: London, British Library, MSS MadSoc A22-25; Boyce, *Cathedral Music*, Vol. 3 (London, 1778): both derived - directly, it would appear - from **D**.
*Bars 110-135*: Croft, *Musica Sacra*, Vol. I (London, 1724): generally following **B**, but with some rhythmic smoothing, especially at feminine endings, and other signs of editorial intervention.

# EDITORIAL PROCEDURE

Prefatory staves show original clefs, key-signatures, time-signatures and first notes. Notes, rests and accidentals printed small, and crossed ties, are editorial. The accidental convention has been modernized by the use of the natural sign - not found in the earliest of the sources - in addition to the sharp and flat, and by the tacit elimination of redundant accidentals. Barring has been systematized. Naming of parts is editorial except where noted in the Commentary; other editorial directions are enclosed in square brackets. Spelling and punctuation have been modernized.

In Morley's settings of the Funeral Sentences none of the vocal material is entirely trustworthy in matters of detail. The organ-book, **E** - the earliest of all the sources - has therefore been generally relied on for the pitch of the outer vocal parts (though not always for their rhythms, since it sometimes gives long notes where the vocal parts have repeated notes); the inner parts are necessarily composite. Furthermore, no two of the sources agree on the underlay, which is often unclear or ambiguous. This problem is compounded by the fact that Morley's text was that of the 1552 Book of Common Prayer, which differs considerably in places from the 1662 text. The present edition therefore offers a conjectural reconstruction of the underlay, in a style likely to have been adopted in 1695 by a musician with a sensitive awareness of Tudor choral music. (Purcell certainly possessed such an awareness, as witness the transcriptions he made in Fitzwilliam Music MS 88 of works by Tudor and Jacobean composers - scoring them up from the Barnard printed part-books expressly in order to clarify their underlay.) Variants affecting only the underlay, and rhythmic variants - repeated or held notes - which are in turn occasioned solely by underlay variants, are not recorded in the Commentary.

In Purcell's setting of "Thou knowest, Lord" **F** and **G** have been treated as the copy-text. The main variant readings, nearly all of which affect cadences or the approach to them (bars 124, 126 and 133), could all plausibly have arisen from revisions superimposed on original readings in the autograph score, and it is perfectly possible that **A**, **F**, **G** and **H** were all copied from it either directly or at no more than one remove.

# ACKNOWLEDGMENTS

I wish to thank the libraries and librarians who have, by their unfailing helpfulness and courtesy, done much to make the present edition possible, and who have kindly permitted the publication of documents in their keeping. I am also grateful to Andrew Pinnock, who first engaged my interest in the Old English March, and to Dr Maurice Byrne, who gave helpful advice concerning certain aspects of its transcription. Finally, I must acknowledge a particular debt of gratitude to the Leverhulme Foundation, whose award of a Fellowship made it possible for me to take the year of sabbatical leave during which I worked on the Funeral Music for Queen Mary and other research projects.

BRUCE WOOD
*University of Wales: Bangor*
*Spring 1996*

# FUNERAL MUSIC FOR QUEEN MARY

Edited and reconstructed by Bruce Wood

## THE OLD ENGLISH MARCH

TRADITIONAL
Transcribed by Bruce Wood

THE VOLUNTARY OR PREPARATION *(to be played once only)*

THE MARCH *(to be repeated ad lib.)*

CODA *(once only)*

# THE QUEEN'S FAREWELL

THOMAS TOLLETT ( *d.*1696)
Edited by Bruce Wood

# THE QUEEN'S FAREWELL

JAMES PAISIBLE ( *d.*1720)
Edited by Bruce Wood

# THE QUEEN'S FUNERAL MARCH

HENRY PURCELL
Edited by Bruce Wood

# FUNERAL SENTENCES

## THE FIRST DIRGE ANTHEM

*To be sung in procession from the entrance of the church*

THOMAS MORLEY (1557/8 - 1602)
Edited by Bruce Wood

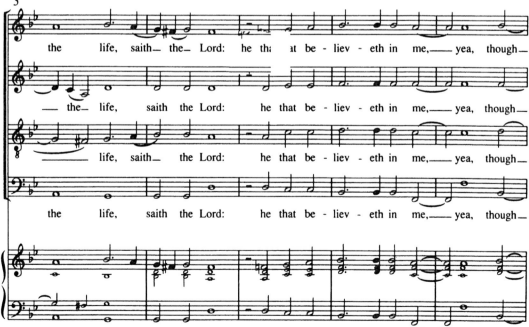

6

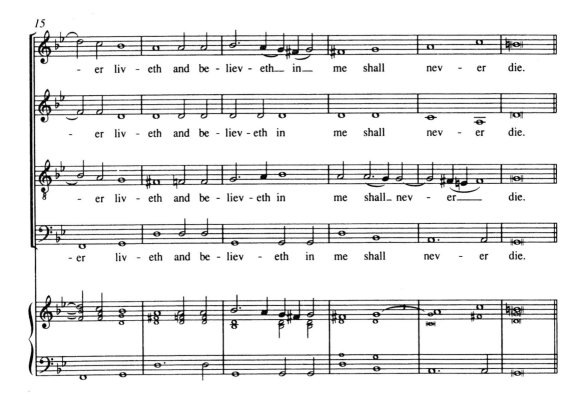

21

I know___ that my Re - deem - er liv - eth, and that he___ shall__ stand, shall

I know___ that my Re - deem - er liv - eth, and that he___ shall stand

I know___ that my Re - deem - er liv - eth, and that he___ shall__ stand, shall__

I know___ that my Re - deem - er liv - eth, and that he___ shall__ stand at the

26

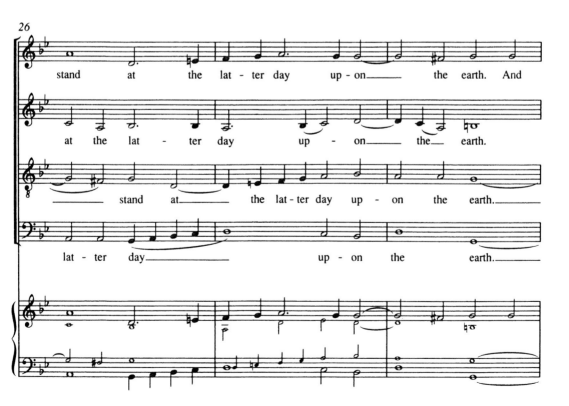

stand at the lat - ter day up - on___ the earth. And

at the lat - ter day up - on___ the___ earth.

___ stand at___ the lat - ter day up - on the earth.___

lat - ter day___ up - on the earth.___

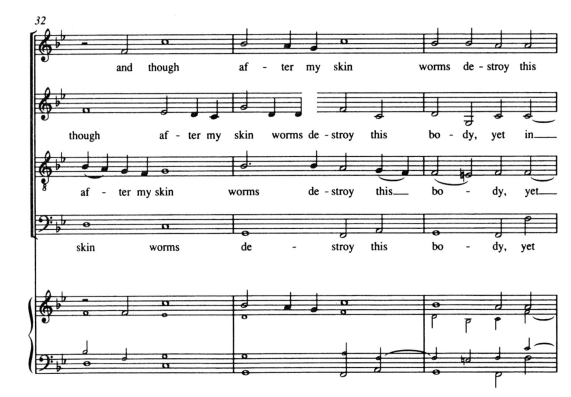

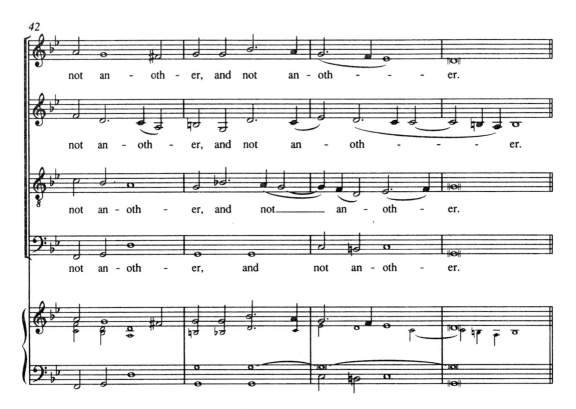

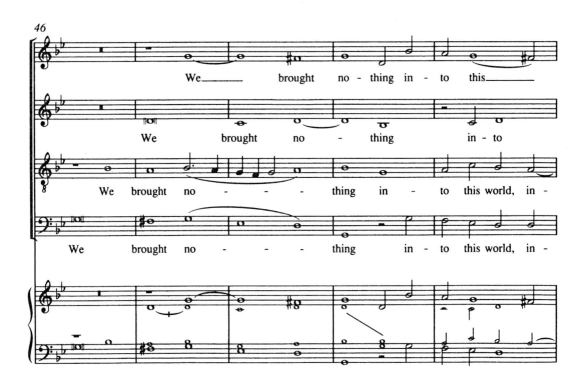

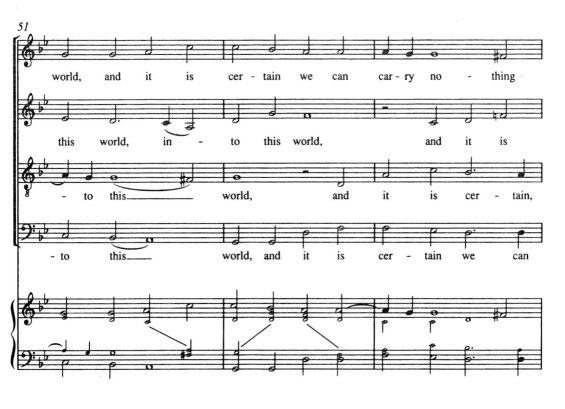

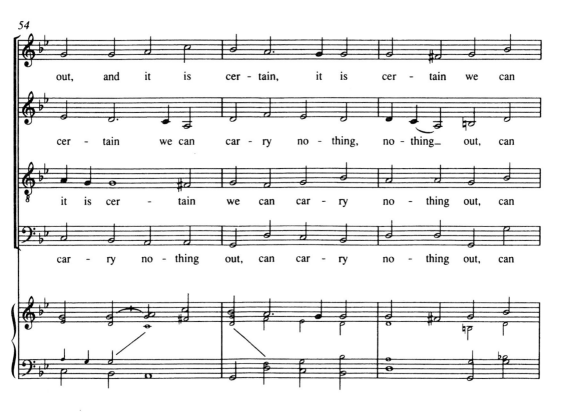

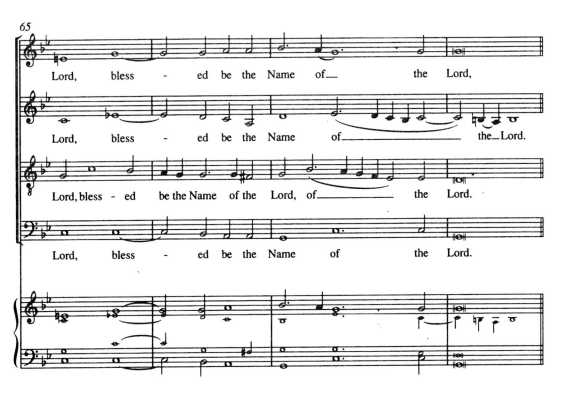

65

Lord, bless - ed be the Name of____ the Lord,

Lord, bless - ed be the Name of_____ the_Lord.

Lord, bless - ed be the Name of the Lord, of_____ the Lord.

Lord, bless - ed be the Name of the Lord.

# THE SECOND DIRGE ANTHEM

*To be sung at the grave*

THOMAS MORLEY
Edited by Bruce Wood

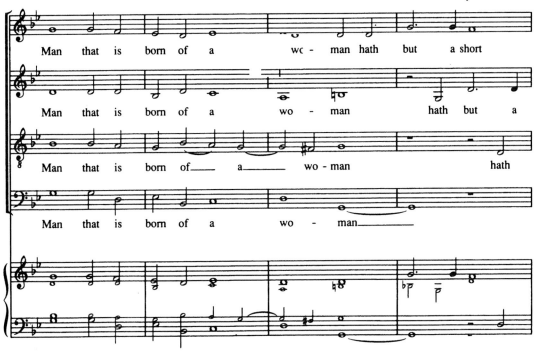

Man that is born of a wo - man hath but a short

Man that is born of a wo - man hath but a

Man that is born of____ a_____ wo - man hath

Man that is born of a wo - man_____

14

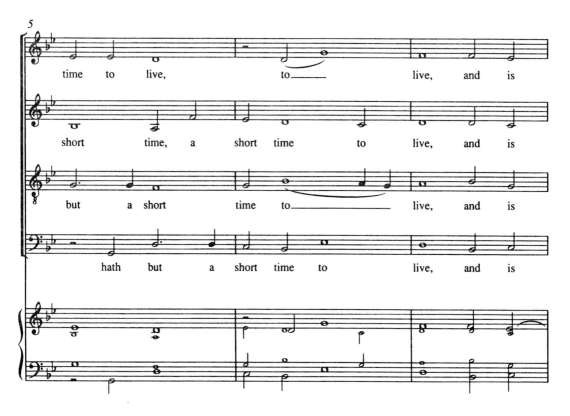

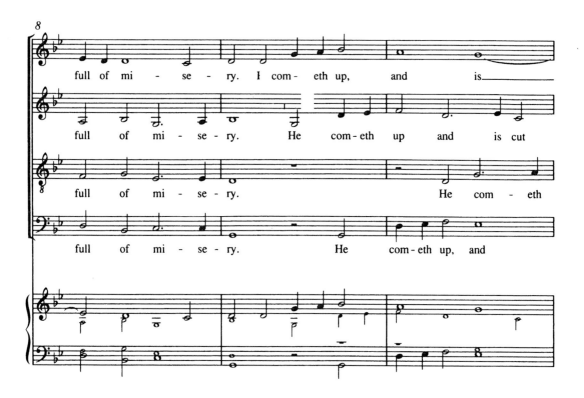

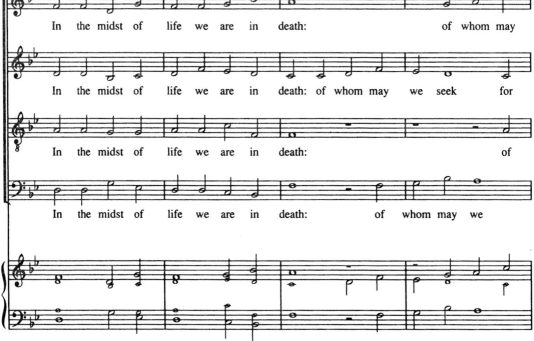

In the midst of life we are in death: of whom may

In the midst of life we are in death: of whom may we seek for

In the midst of life we are in death: of

In the midst of life we are in death: of whom may we

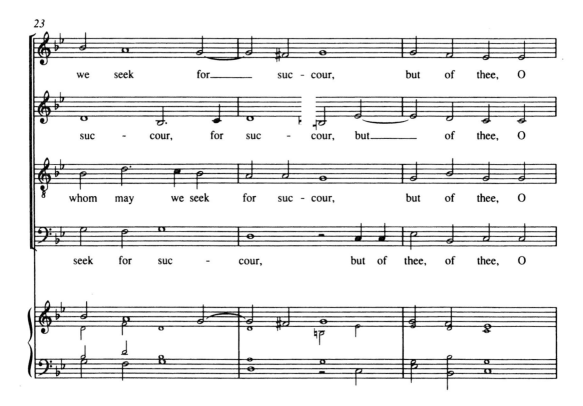

we seek for_____ suc - cour, but of thee, O

suc - cour, for suc - cour, but_____ of thee, O

whom may we seek for suc - cour, but of thee, O

seek for suc - cour, but of thee, of thee, O

HENRY PURCELL
Edited by Bruce Wood

Thou know-est, Lord, the se-crets of our hearts; shut not, shut not thy

Thou know-est, Lord, the se-crets of our hearts; shut not, shut not thy

Thou know-est, Lord, the se-crets of our hearts; shut not, shut not thy

Thou know-est, Lord, the se-crets of our hearts; shut not, shut not thy

mer-ci-ful ears un - to our pray - e but spare us, Lord, spare us,

mer-ci-ful ears un - to our pray - er; but spare us, Lord, spare us,

mer-ci-ful ears un - to our pray - er; but spare us, Lord, spare us,

mer-ci-ful ears un - to our pray - er; but spare us, Lord, spare us,

# CANZONA

*As it was sounded in the Abbey after the anthem*

HENRY PURCELL
Edited by Bruce Wood

# THE THIRD DIRGE ANTHEM

*To be sung after the earth has been cast upon the body*

THOMAS MORLEY
Edited by Bruce Wood

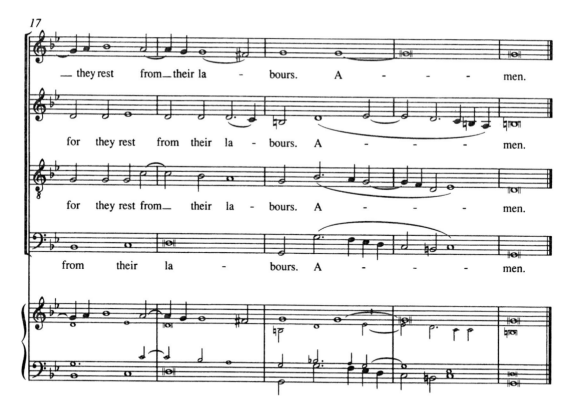

— they rest from their la - bours. A - - - men.

for they rest from their la - bours. A - - - men.

for they rest from their la - bours. A - - - men.

from their la - bours. A - - - men.

*Ossie* for bars 16 - 17
Sources **B, C, E**

— the Spi - rit, for they rest from—

— la - bours, for they rest

la - bours, for they rest from—

la - bours, from their la -

Sources **A, D**

— the Spi-rit, for— they rest from

— la - bours, for— they rest

la - bours, for— they rest from

la - bours, their la -

# A NOTE ON THE TEXTUAL COMMENTARY

*Abbreviations*: Tr, treble; CT, counter-tenor; T, tenor; B, bass; Ob, oboe; Bsn, bassoon; Tpt, trumpet; Org, organ; lh, left hand; rh, right hand; *br*, breve; *sbr*, semibreve; *m*, minim; *cr*, crotchet; *q*, quaver; *sq*, semiquaver; *cr.*, dotted crotchet (*etc*).

*Pitch* is shown by means of standard Helmholtz notation (thus octaves reading upwards from 8-foot pitch are C, c, c′, c″, and each octave symbol remains in force from C to the B above).

*System of reference*: 44.T.4-5: *m* (♭)e, *m* c **AB** means that in bar 44 of the tenor part, from the fourth symbol (note, including tied notes, or rest) to the fifth, the printed reading is replaced in sources **A** and **B** by a minim e (rendered flat by the key-signature) and a minim c.

# TEXTUAL COMMENTARY

*The Old English March*

**TF**  Thomas Fisher, *Warlike Directions* (**TF¹**: 1634 edition; **TF²**: 1643 edition)

**RH**  Randle Holme, Lbl MS Harl. 2034

**HW**  Horace Walpole, *Catalogue of Royal and Noble Authors*

"Within the March are 9. severall lines, or ranks, which must be ... distinctly beaten, dividing line from line, by a certain distance of time ... There is also a preparation to the March which is only to be beaten once, and no more, at the beginning of the March." The March is printed in nine separate lines, and the Preparation in a single line divided by a full stop. **TF**

In **RH** the two phrases of the Preparation (there termed Voluntarie) are written in one line - divided by a comma in the mnemonic version, but with no rests included in the transcription into musical notation which is written immediately above; the fifth and sixth phrases of the March, and the eighth and ninth, are likewise written in the mnemonic version in single lines, each divided by a comma. In **HW** the Voluntary, the fifth and sixth and the eighth and ninth lines of the March are printed as single lines of notes without intermediate rests. It is

notable that each of the lines thus linked to the preceding one begins with a left-hand or anacrusial stroke. ·

In this edition the note-values of **RH** and **HW** have been halved, so as to secure equivalence with the note-values of Purcell's March. It is these halved note-values which are referred to in the list of variants which follows.

1.1: plain quaver only **RH, HW**
2.1: crotchet followed by a comma, then next crotchet **RH**; crotchet followed immediately by next crotchet **HW**
3.1: omitted **TF²**
7.4: plain stroke only **TF²**
13.5-6: single ruff only **RH**; minim with ruff **HW**
14.1: plain stroke only (not long stroke), followed by a comma and next stroke **RH**; plain crotchet followed immediately by next crotchet **HW**
15.2-4: omitted **HW**
19.3, 6: full, not half ruff **RH, HW**
20.1: plain stroke only (not long stroke), followed by a comma and next stroke **RH**; plain crotchet followed immediately by next crotchet **HW**
21.5: followed by additional ruff **RH**

*Paisible and Tollett: Oboe Marches*

Naming of parts: First Treble, Second
Treble, Tenor (Paisible only), Bass.

*Paisible*:
4.Ob1, 6.Ob2, 6.Bsn, 8.Bsn: *sbr*
7.T-Ob.1-2: slurred together

*Purcell: March*

Bars 4, 8, 12, 16: omitted, with a double
bar-line after bars 3, 6, 9, 12.

The various manuscripts of the theatre
version of the March differ in small details,
both from the funeral version and from each
other; they all agree, however, in replacing
each of the internal double bar-lines in the
funeral version with a bar's rest.

19-20: first-time version editorial.


*Morley and Purcell: Dirge Anthems*

A    *Ob* Tenbury MS 859 (complete)
B    *Lbl* Harl. MS 7337 (Morley only)
C    *Lbl* Add. MS 5054 (variants listed
     for Morley only)
D    *Lbl* MSS MadSoc A52-55 (Morley
     only)
E    *Ojc* MS 315 (Morley only)
F    *Och* MS 794 (Purcell only)
G    *Lbl* Add. MS 31444 (Purcell only)
H    Lbl Harl. MS 7340 (Purcell only)


*The First Dirge Anthem*
1.all: *sbr* **A**
6.B.1-2: *m. cr* **A**
9.B.2: 8ve lower **B**
13.T.1-3: *sbr* c', *m* d' **D**
16.T.1: o **B**
16.T.2 (on new page): o **A**
17.B.2-3: crotchets G A (♭)B C **A**
18.Org-rh.2, Org-lh.2: each note marked
with two staccato-like dots side by side
(indicating repeated notes in the vocal
parts) **E**
19.T.2-3: *m* ♮ e **B**

20.Org-rh: *sbr.* ♮ b', *m* ♭ b' **E**
21.T.2-22.T.4: g g (♭)b a g **C**
22.Org-lh.1: *m*-rest **E**
23.Org-rh.2: (♭)b' **E**
24.T.3: a **AB**
25.CT.1: *cr* f', *cr* ♮ e' **BC**
25.T.4: *cr* a, *cr* g **A**
26.Tr.3: o **BC**
26.B, Org-lh.3-4: *cr. q* **BCE**; 26.B.5-6:
*cr. q* **C** (presumably setting and painting
the word *rise* in the 1552 text)
27.T.2: o **C**
28.Org-rh.3: as in bar 18
30.Org-rh.2: as in bar 18
34.Org-rh.1: as in bar 18
35.B.1-2, org-lh.1-2: *m. cr* **BDE**
(creating an ungrammatical six-four chord
on the second beat)
37.B.1: 8ve higher **A**
38.Tr.2: *cr* (♭)b', *cr* a **A**
38.B.2: *cr* G, *cr* A **A**
38.B.4: *cr* A *cr* G **A**
41.B.1: 8ve higher **A**
42.T.3: *m. cr* **B**
43.CT.1: o **A**
43.B.1: 8ve higher **A**
44.CT.4, 45.CT.1: omitted, and
remainder thus two beats early **A**
44.T.4-5: *m* (♭)e, *m* c **AB**
45.CT.2-3: *m* a **B**
52.B.4: d **BCD**
52.Org-rh.3: as in bar 18
53.CT.4: d' **D**
53.T.3-4: *m* (♭)b, *c* a, *c* a **A**; *m m* **B**
55.Tr.3: a' **CD**
56.T.1-2: *m.* a, *cr* g **B**
56.T.3-4: *m. cr* **B**; all other sources give
bald consecutive octaves with the treble
58.CT.3-4: *m. cr* **B**
59.CT.2: o **B**
59.CT.3, 60.CT.1: b (no accidental) **B**
60.CT.3: a note low **D**
61.Org-rh.2: as in bar 18 **E**
62.CT.3-5: a third higher **B**
62.Org-rh, lh.4: as in bar 18 **E**

63.B.1 - 64.B.2: *m* F, then *m sbr* tied to *m cr cr*, all f **A**
66.CT.4: c′ **B**
67.CT.2 - 69.CT.1: *sbr.* (♭)e′, m c′, *br* d′ **B**
67.CT.4-5: *m* c′, *m* c′ **A**
68.B: 8ve higher **A**


*The Second Dirge Anthem*
3.CT.2: o **B**
4.CT.4: c′ **A**
4.T.1: *sbr* g **B**
5.Tr.3 - 6.Tr.1: *m* d′, *m* f′, *m* (♭)e′ **D**
5.CT.3: *m* a, *m* d′ **BD**
6.CT.1: *m*-rest **BD**
7.Tr.1: ♮ to f′ **D**
8.Tr.1-3: *sbr.* d′ **B**
8.Tr.2: (♭)e′ **C**
8.CT.4, 9.CT.1: g g **C**
11.B.4: **B A**
13.T.3-4: *m. cr* **ABC**
13.B.1: *m* G, tied back **A**
16.T.1: *cr* ( )b (tied back), *cr* g **B**
17.T.2: (♭)b **AD**
18.CT.1: d′ **CD**
19.CT.3: d′ **BCD**
19.T.3: (♭)b **C**
19.Org-rh.1: as in bar 18 of First Dirge Anthem **E**
23.CT: *sbr.* d′, m (♭)e′ **A**
23.CT.2-3: *m* d′, *m* g **BC**
23.T.2-3: *cr cr* d′, *m* c′ **A**
23.B.2: ♯ to f **A**
24.CT.2: o **A**
25.Org-rh.2: as in bar 18 of First Dirge Anthem **E**
27.Tr.3: ♯ to f′ **A**
29.Tr.3: o **A**
30.Org-rh.2: as in bar 18 of First Dirge Anthem **E**
32.T.3: *cr* (♭)b, *cr* c′ **CD**
32.B.1: *m* c (tied back), *m* g **C**
33.CT.1: d′ **AB**
35.Tr, Org-rh.1: ♯ to f′ **AE**

36.T.3: (♭)b **D**
41.Tr: f′ **A**
42-67.Org: notated at sounding pitch **F**
43.T.3-4: *m* c′ **G**
53.Tr.2: d″ **A**
54.B.3-4: 8ve lower **H**
56.Tr.3: *m* c ″ **A**
56.T.3-4: *cr* d′, *cr* c′ **AFH**
57.B.2: f **A**
58.Tr.1-2: *m. cr* **AG**
58.T.3-4: *m m* **FH**
58.B.1-2, Org-lh.1: 8ve lower **G**
58.B.3-4: *m m* **A**
61.CT.3: g′ **A**
62.B.2-3: *sbr.* d, tied back **AG**
62-63.bc: notes (though not all the necessary ties) provided, on same stave as vocal bass **FH**
63.T.4 - 65.T.1: underlaid *for any pains of death* **AFGH**; the editorial emendation, probably conforming to Purcell's intentions since it significantly clarifies the homophony in bars 64-65, follows Croft's *Musica Sacra*
63.Org-lh.4: lower note on upstem (♭) e **G**
65.Tr.2-3: *sbr*, slurred to next note and underlaid *from* **A**
65.CT.3-4: underlaid *fall* (no slur) **A**
65.CT.3-4: *m.* c′, *cr* d′ **G**
65.T.4-5: *m* a **GH**
66.CT.1: *m. cr*, underlaid *from thee* **A**
66.all.2-3: *sbr* **A**


*Purcell: Canzona*
1: time-signature **C**
5.Tpt3: ♯ to the third note cancelled, and ♯ added to the fourth note, by a later hand
6.Tpt3.4: c′
23.Tpt3: d′ d′ d′ d′
30.Tpt3: last two notes originally f′ f′; a′ a′ added by a later hand, which left the original reading uncancelled.

*The Third Dirge Anthem*
2.Tr.2, Org-rh.2: ♯ to f′ **AD**
3.B.2: ♯ to f **ABE**;   added later **D**
4.CT.1: f′ **B**
5.Tr.4: o **A**
6.T.1-2: *sbr* tied to *cr* g, cr f **A**; *m* g, *m.* g, *cr* f **B**
6.B.1: *m.* g, *cr* G **D**
8.Tr: blank (no rest) **A**
8.CT: *sbr* c′, *sbr* (♭) e′ (tied forward) **D**
8.Org-rh: *sbr sbr*, both (♭) e′ **E**
9.Tr.2: *m* c′, underlaid *write* **A**
9.Org-rh: blank, then *sbr* c″ tied forward **E**
10.Tr.1: (♭) b′ **A**
11.Org-lh.1: as in bar 18 of First Dirge Anthem **E**
12.B.2: 8ve higher **D**
13.Org-lh.1: as in bar 18 of First Dirge Anthem **E**
14-17: *that* instead of *for* in text (as in 1552 Prayer Book) **A**
14.CT.2: d′ **A**
15.Tr.2-3: *cr cr m* all on a′ **D**
15.B.4-5: 8ve higher **D**
15.Org-rh.2-3: *sbr* a′ **E**
18.CT.2-4: *m.* d′, *cr* c′, *m* a **A**
19.T.2: ♮ b **A**

*Ossie*: neither version is satisfactory as it stands. In **AD** the movement of the bass shadows that of the tenor and is in turn shadowed by that of the treble. In **BCE** the relationship between tenor and bass is ungrammatical, with a suspended fourth quitted by upward leap onto an unprepared seventh - two solecisms against which Morley himself explicitly warns in *A Plaine and Easie Introduction to Practicall Musick*. But the tenor of **BCE** fits happily with the other parts as given in **AD**. The confusion may have arisen from a revision by the composer and the subsequent mingling of a set of parts containing the revised version with another containing the unrevised one.